CHESAPEAKE BAY

A Picture Book to Remember Her by

CRESCENT BOOKS
NEW YORK

CLB 876
© 1985 Colour Library Books Ltd, Godalming, Surrey, England.
All rights reserved.
This 1991 edition published by Crescent Books,
distributed by Outlet Book Company, Inc, a Random House Company,
225 Park Avenue South, New York, New York 10003.
Text filmsetting by Acesetters Ltd, Richmond, Surrey, England.
Printed in Hong Kong.
ISBN 0 517 477866
8 7 6 5 4 3 2

Back in the early days of the 20th century, when you could say such things and not offend anybody, a local scholar wrote that in the Chesapeake Bay area, "the women are the most beautiful in the world because of their steady diet of seafood." Though almost everybody agreed with his statement of effect, not everyone agreed with the cause of it. But when anyone is invited to a Chesapeake Bay crab feast or an oyster roast or to share the glory of a diamond-back terrapin, they hardly ever accept because they think it will make them beautiful. Nothing can make you happier, though. Sometimes not even the company of beautiful women.

Probably more than anything else, the poor man had run out of superlatives about the Bay and its surrounding Tidewater Country. People have been enthusiastic about the Chesapeake since a Spanish explorer arrived in 1573 and reported an astounding number of rivers and harbors. He didn't bother to count them all, but more patient explorers have identified about 40 different rivers, all of which, except the Susquehanna which wanders down from Pennsylvania and empties into the bay not far from Baltimore, are navigable for a considerable distance. There are hundreds of other smaller rivers and creeks, most of which lead to very comfortable harbors. Officially, there are about 90 harbors between Norfolk, Virginia, at the southern end of the Chesapeake and the Chesapeake and Delaware Canal at the northern end. It's the biggest inland body of water on America's Atlantic coast, stretching almost 170 nautical miles from north to south and ranging from about three miles wide near the mouth of the Potomac River to as much as 23 miles wide at the point where Maryland and Virginia meet on the Delmarva Peninsula.

Though it is as important today as it has ever been, providing access to important ports like Norfolk, Newport News and Baltimore, a great deal of American history has unfolded there. The first English settlement in North America was established at Jamestown, not far from the Bay, on the James River in 1607. In 1634, the brother of Lord Baltimore established the first settlement in Maryland on the St. Mary's River. The battle of Yorktown that ended the Revolutionary War was fought along the banks of another river leading to the Chesapeake, the York. And, of course, the Capital City of Washington was built on the shore of the Potomac, yet another river that finds its way to the sea through the Chesapeake Bay.

The Star Spangled Banner was written at the entrance to Baltimore Harbor during the War of 1812, when the City of Baltimore already referred to itself as "The Queen of The Chesapeake." And in the Civil War, the great clash of the ironclads, the Monitor and the Merrimac, made history at Hampton Roads at the other end of the Bay.

Hampton Roads, Virginia, is formed by the meeting of the James, Nanesmond and Elizabeth Rivers and the lower Bay. There are very few better natural harbors in the world than this one that includes the ports of Norfolk, Newport News, Portsmouth and Hampton. More than 5000 ships a year sail from there and it's home to the largest American Naval base in the world, home port for most of the Atlantic Fleet.

But what happens on the Bay is sometimes overshadowed by what happens along its shores. On the Eastern Shore of Maryland, for instance, where millionaires from other places have bought and restored magnificent Colonial mansions and live side-by-side with people whose families seem to have lived there forever and who bear the traits of independence that put even New England Yankees in the shade, they still hunt the descendants of eight pairs of English red foxes that were imported in 1730. And not just on the Eastern Shore. The foxes range all over the Tidewater Country of Maryland and Virginia, despite the number of hunt clubs that have been established to make them an endangered species.

It's also terrific duck hunting country, and there are very few places along the Bay's more than 5000 miles of shoreline that are far from a duck blind or two where men wait in the chilly dampness for a flock of mallards or pintails or canvasbacks.

It's a fisherman's paradise, too. Some 500,000 people a year go out on the Bay for the fun of it. They fish from small rowboats and palatial cabin cruisers or from pilings along the shore. Some others, who prefer to keep on the move, enjoy the Bay in fast, 22-foot star boats, far and away the most popular sailing experience in a place that includes nearly 50 major yachting centers, all of which are host to impressive schedules of sailing races which, in turn, attract an impressive number of competitors.

But best of all the things there are to do around the Chesapeake, there is nothing quite like just looking. There are those beautiful women on seafood diets, of course, and there are the fascinating weathered faces of the Bay Watermen who provide the food for those diets. And the landscapes and seascapes give a backdrop to people-watching that can't be matched anywhere.

Facing page: the *USF Constellation* in Baltimore.

Facing page: the Baltimore City Hall, which was built in the 1870s and has recently been lovingly restored to its original splendor. This page: the wide, brick walkways of the Inner Harbor, a favorite venue for shopping and dining.

Top: Baltimore City Hall, with its cast-iron dome. Remaining pictures: Inner Harbor with the *USF Constellation*. Launched in 1797, the *Constellation* became, just two years later, the first American ship to capture a major prize.

Facing page: the view along Charles Street to the distant Washington Monument. This 178-foot-tall column is surmounted by a statue of Washington and can be climbed by 228 steps. It was begun in 1815 and was, therefore, the first major memorial to Washington. This page: the colorful setting of Inner Harbor.

9

Top: the Power Plant on Inner Harbor, a fantastic entertainment complex of electric delights. Left: the Flag House, home of Mary Pickersgill, who made the actual flag which inspired the National Anthem. Above: a house in Chesapeake City. Facing page: an old building in Fells Point.

ANCHORS
CHAIN
SEINE.

CANVAS
COVERS
CORKS

ROPE, CANVAS, METALS

CHINA SEA MARINE
TRADING CO.

Capt. S.D. BUNKER   H. Wm OLIVER
FINEST
SAIL & STEAMSHIP
· SALVAGE ·

SEXTANTS & OCTANTS
INSTRUMENTS
Telescopes
CHARTS
FLAGS
PENNANTS

11

These pages: Annapolis: (left) State House; (below) Chase-Lloyd House; (bottom) Hammond-Harwood House; facing page: (top) Paca House; (bottom left) Governor's Mansion; (bottom right) London Town Publik House. Overleaf: Annapolis City Docks and nearby scenes.

These pages: Annapolis; (above) Main Street; (right) the domed Chapel and Buchanan House at the Naval Academy and (facing page) the dome of the State House and a typical street.

16

The United States Naval Academy (these pages) stands in Annapolis and has been training officers for the Navy since 1845: (top) the ice rink in Dahlgren Hall; (left) Nimitz Library. Above: Michelson Hall and (facing page) the interior of the Chapel. Overleaf: Annapolis.

Top: Main Street in St. Michaels. Above left: the pale sands of North Beach. Left: a lifting bridge at Tilghman Harbor. Above: a sleek powerboat in St. Michaels Harbor. Facing page: (top) the Maritime Museum at St Michaels; (bottom left) the Benjamin Stevens House in Easton and (bottom right) Main Street, St. Michaels. Overleaf: sunset over the Blackwater National Wildlife Refuge.

22

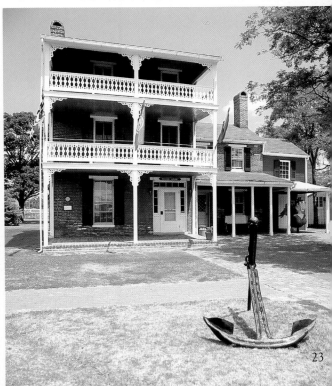

23

Previous pages: sunset near Cambridge with insets: (top left) scene near Thomas; (bottom left) the Courthouse, Easton; (top right) Blackwater Wildlife Refuge and (bottom right) Washington St. Easton. These pages: the past recreated at: (top left) Farthing's Ordinary, (left, above and top) the Dedication Ceremony for the Charter of Maryland and (facing page center left and bottom right) a plantation, all in St Marys and (facing page bottom left and top) Sotterly, Hollywood. Overleaf: sunset at Lookout Point with, as insets: (top and bottom left) Colton Point and (right) the *Dove*, a replica of one of the ships which brought Maryland's first settlers in 1634.

This page: catching and processing crabs at Crisfield, center of the Chesapeake Bay seafood industry. Facing page: (top and bottom right) Lookout Point and (bottom left) Deal Island. Overleaf: Tangier Island with, as insets: (top left and top right) Tangier Island; (bottom left) Kings Creek Marina, near Cape Charles and (bottom right) Onancock.

Top, above and facing page, top: Popes Creek Plantation, the recreated birthplace of George Washington. Left: Little Oyster Creek. Facing page, bottom: Stratford Hall, the 18th-century birthplace of Robert E. Lee.

These pages: Popes Creek Plantation, where George Washington was born and spent his childhood, was a typical tidewater plantation. Today, the site has been rebuilt to represent such a complex with gardens and reproductions of a kitchen house and an upper class home as well as working colonial farm buildings. The outline of the great man's birthplace is picked out in oyster shells, though the foundations have been buried to protect them.

These pages: Stratford Hall, home of the Lee family, which figures prominently in the nation's history. Above: the nursery; (top center) the Great House; (top right) the kitchen; (bottom right) the blue bedroom; (right) the parlor.

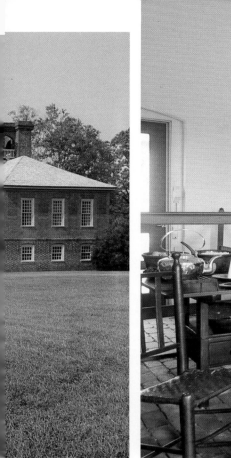

When Lord Cornwallis surrendered his entire army to the Americans in 1781 after the siege of Yorktown, American independence was assured. Far left and below: cannon on the battlefield. Left: the Victory Monument. Bottom and facing page bottom: Moore House, where the terms of surrender were negotiated on October 18th.

Williamsburg (these pages and overleaf) is one of the great historic sites of the nation. A large section of the town has been restored to its 18th-century condition as buildings are renovated or rebuilt and costumed staff act out the life of days gone by.

Near the banks of the James River is the Georgian mansion of Carter's Grove (these pages), built in 1750-1753. In the early 1700s, Robert 'King' Carter, the richest of the Virginia planters, bought the 1,400 acres of land upon which his grandson, Carter Burwell, built the three-story mansion house. Fine workmanship in loblolly-pine and walnut helps make this, arguably, the most beautiful house in America.

Jamestown Festival Park stands next to the site where 104 settlers arrived in 1607 to found the first permanent English settlement on the continent. The park boasts full scale replicas of the three ships which brought the settlers as well as of their homes and the tobacco fields which brought them prosperity.

These pages: the great amusement park of Busch Gardens, where the past of four countries is evoked alongside a wide array of rides and attractions.

After the British burnt Washington in 1814, Fort Monroe became the largest stone fortress in the United States: (above) the Casement Museum; (top) Chapel of the Centurion; (inset top) a 12-pounder howitzer and (inset bottom) the Lincoln Gun. Right: a cannon at Yorktown.

THE LINCOLN GUN

CAST IN 1860, THIS WAS THE
FIRST 15-INCH RODMAN GUN. ITS
RANGE WAS MORE THAN FOUR
MILES. WEIGHT OF THE PROJECTILE
WAS OVER 300 LBS. DURING CIVIL
WAR IT WAS USED TO BOMBARD
CONFEDERATE BATTERIES ON
SEWELLS POINT. THE GUN WAS
NAMED FOR PRESIDENT LINCOLN
IN MARCH 1862.

1969

The third of a million Virginians who live in Norfolk (these pages and overleaf) inhabit one of the most varied cities in America. For, although the industrial power of the city is undeniable, culture and art also take their place in the make-up of the city. It is the great Naval Dockyards, however, which are its best known feature. Warships are a common sight in the city off whose shores the Merrimack met the Monitor in 1862, in the first battle between ironclads.

The shores of Virginia (these pages) have been popular with vacationers for generations. The Chesapeake Bay Bridge-Tunnel (above) reaches 17 miles across the mouth of Chesapeake Bay. It includes some two miles of causeway and 12 miles of trestled roadway together with two mile-long tunnels which allow the largest ships to pass into the Bay.

Top: an example of the private frontage along the coast at Virginia Beach. Above: Virginia Beach, Ocean Front. Right: at 157 feet, New Cape Henry Lighthouse is the tallest cast-iron lighthouse in the country. Despite its name, the lighthouse is far from new, having been constructed in 1881 to replace the Old Lighthouse of 1791.